PRINCIPLES OF BRAIN MANAGEMENT

D0831399

PRINCIPLES OF BRAIN MANAGEMENT

A PRACTICAL APPROACH TO MAKING THE MOST OF YOUR BRAIN

ILCHI LEE

BEST Life Media
6560 Highway 179, Suite 114
Sedona, AZ 86351
www.bestlifemedia.com
1-877-504-1106

Copyright © 2007 by Ilchi Lee

All rights reserved. No part of this book may be produced or transmitted in any form or by any means, electronic or mechanical, including photocopying, recording, or by any information storage or retrieval system, without permission in writing from the publisher.

First paperback edition: September 2007
Library of Congress Control Number: 2007936251

ISBN-10: 0–9799388–0–5
ISBN-13: 978–0–9799388–0–1

If you are unable to order this book from your local bookseller,
you may order through www.amazon.com or www.bestlifemedia.com.

The brain gives the heart its sight.
The heart gives the brain its vision.

—*Rob Kall*, biofeedback pioneer

Contents

2. Flexing Your Gray Matter

3. Cleaning Out the Attic

4. Connecting the Dots

5. Seeing the Big Picture

Appendix

Introduction

Your Brain Is Your Life

Have you ever stopped to realize that you owe everything you are to your brain?

If someone asks you who you are, what do you say? Maybe you say something like, "My name is John. I am a twenty-seven-year-old man of African descent, and I currently work as an elementary school teacher in Dallas, Texas." Instinctively, you and John both know that there is much more to you. John loves most of all to be in the presence of great art. The hair on the nape of his neck stands up when he smells freshly fallen rain. Both of you have experienced a great range of love and suffering throughout your life. How can one name or one identity sum up all of this?

All these things do have one thing in common, however—they were generated through the brain. John's brain enabled him to become a school teacher, and it is through his brain that he feels awe when standing before a powerful painting. A symphony of sensory input and memory within his brain gives rise to his reaction to freshly fallen rain. It is also within his brain that he stores his definition of what it means to be a man, twenty-seven years old, and African-American.

In some sense, you could say that you are your brain. Or, at the very least, the brain is the instrument through which you experience all reality. And it is through it that you interact with reality—in every emotional reaction, in every choice that you make, and in every dream that you dream. Everything you ever have been or will become is because of your brain.

The conditions of your life at the present moment are also dependent on the condition of your brain. If you love the conditions of your life, you must use your brain to help you maintain that life. If you want to change the conditions of your life, it will also require effective use of your brain.

You Are the Master of Your Brain

The great news is that you have infinite power to change and refine your brain. A few decades back, scientists thought that people could have very little influence over their brains. It was assumed that by the time people reached adulthood their brain connections were permanently and indelibly in place. In childhood, one might be able to exert some influence over the development of the brain, but for the most part these things were genetically determined. It was thought that the old adage "You can't teach an old dog new tricks" was literally true.

More recently, scientists have discovered that the opposite is true. There is a quality to the brain called neuroplasticity that allows you, right up to the end of your life, to restructure and adapt your brain according to your needs. You can learn new things and adapt to new environments, even in extreme old age.

You may protest that the "old dog" does seem a little resistant to "new tricks." Common experience would suggest that young children learn and adapt more quickly than adults, especially older adults.

This is, in fact, often the case, but I would suggest that it is partly a matter of choice, rather than a predetermined trait of the brain. There may indeed be some biological barriers to overcome as we get older. The brain's connections do become denser and slower as we fill the brain with the experiences and knowledge of a lifetime. However, most people lose a great deal of their neuroplasticity simply because they choose not to use it. For that reason, I encourage you to use and challenge your brain as much as possible. You will find that, in the end, developing your brain is the same as leading a vital, fulfilling lifestyle.

An Evolutionary Masterpiece

You can look at your brain as a microcosm that contains everything you have been and holds the potential of everything you will become. The brain is unique when compared with other organs because it is the only one that exerts influence on the world outside your body as well as inside your body. It is also the only organ that can be used to understand itself, and it is the only organ that can modify itself.

You already know that your brain holds and stores many experiences from your past. Even if you are eighty, you probably still retain some strong memories from your childhood, and even if you haven't ridden a bicycle for many years, you probably could ride one today without much trouble. Yes, some things are forgotten, but there is no doubt that the experiences you have had in the past and the things you learned long ago all have played a role in shaping your brain and making you who you are today.

But did you ever stop to consider that your brain remembers even further back into your past than your childhood? Can you imagine that it holds elements that could go even further back than your conception? This may seem strange at first, but it is really not as mystical as it sounds.

The human brain contains a record of the evolution of sentient life on this planet within its basic structures. When you think of the human brain and its marvelous capabilities, you probably think of all the marvelous creations that come from the human being's highly developed cortical region. This development in the human brain was essential to creating the dominant role we enjoy on the planet. None of the great culture, bustling cities, or life-changing technologies that define our human experience would be possible without the prefrontal cortex of the human brain. But the story does not end there.

All the earlier evolutionary incarnations of the brain are still apparent in the human brain. While the prefrontal cortex of the brain has gotten bigger and more complex, it has never evolved away from its reliance on the other "lower" incarnations of the animal brain. The human brain still contains the emotionally oriented limbic system, which dominates in the brains of other mammals. And it still contains the brain stem, which is the most basic part of the brain, common to all animals with a central nervous system. In fact, this "reptilian" part of the brain is still the most critical to our lives. Without it, our most vital biological functions, like breathing and heartbeat, could not continue.

You could say that all the problems in your life result from disconnection between the ideals created in the cortical region and the impulses of the animal parts of your brain. Your prefrontal cortex is the source of your highest aspirations and the place where you form the ideals by which you live. But the "lower" levels of your brain can easily derail what your prefrontal cortex has determined to be ideal. Emotions generated in the limbic system often lead to behaviors out of line with your ideals, and your brain stem can produce stress responses that undermine, rather than support your personal goals. The main purpose of this book is to help you get the diverse areas of your brain working together, in mutual support, rather than in opposition.

Five Steps to Brain Mastery

The information in the following chapters will lead you to a sense of empowerment over the workings of your brain. The goal is to develop awareness of the role of the brain in your life, to gain an ability to coordinate the various parts of your brain, and ultimately to gain mastery over your brain so that it is working fully in your favor. Apply the principles presented here to your life with honesty and sincerity, and you will discover a new sense of peace and meaning for your life.

The content of this book is based on the Brain Education System Training, which includes the following steps: Brain Sensitizing, Brain Versatilizing, Brain Refreshing, Brain Integrating, and Brain Mastering (see Appendix, page 86). Ultimately, the steps are meant to be practiced simultaneously over the course of a lifetime as you continually revisit and refine each step. However, in the beginning, it is worthwhile to linger on each step to find a solid sense of understanding and proficiency before going on to the next step.

My greatest hope is that the information in these pages will help you find greater happiness and fulfillment in your life. This is really not about brain development in the academic sense. It is not about getting better grades or higher scores on IQ tests. These things are fine, and they may happen as a result of this method. But all that really matters in the end is your overall quality of life. So please use this book well, use your brain well, and uncover the great joy of living that is your human birthright.

1.

Coming Back to Your Senses

Has life's rat race driven you out of your senses? Like a lot of people today, you may feel a general sense of information overload. Your brain may have become hazy, tired—just plain stressed out. The first step in brain management is called **Brain Sensitizing**. Where your brain has become dulled, this step will reawaken your brain and reconnect you to the vibrancy of life.

Manage Your Stress

The ability to manage stress is the holy grail of brain management. Every other attempt to develop and use your brain well can be thwarted if you do not gain some level of control over your stress response. Unmanaged, habitual stress reactions interrupt the learning process, contribute dramatically to brain aging, and are at the root of numerous chronic disease conditions.

First of all, though, you should know that stress is not all bad. It is this process that allows us to respond quickly and effectively in emergency situations. When managed appropriately, the stress response helps stimulate the brain, improving mood and encouraging creative problem solving. Researchers have found that minor amounts of stress, such as that experienced during basic life and occupational challenges, actually improve immune function, while extreme or prolonged stress has the opposite effect.

Continual, prolonged stress response is highly destructive to the brain as well as other organs of the body. The main stress-response hormone, cortisol, can and does kill brain cells, especially in the hippocampus, which is involved in learning and memory formation. Many serious brain-related problems, including attention deficit/hyperactivity disorder (ADHD), Parkinson's disease, and Alzheimer's have been clearly linked to the destructive nature of prolonged exposure to stress hormones.

The stress response is created in the sympathetic nervous system, which sends messages from the brain to the rest of the body, alerting it to the presence of danger. Essentially, it is designed to redirect all energy toward the crisis at hand. Under the influence of stress hormones, the performance of many organs throughout the body is diminished while heart rate increases and blood flow is redirected to the muscles for a rapid fight-or-flight response.

Fortunately, the brain wants to find a state of homeostasis, to achieve balance between excitement and tranquility. This is where the parasympathetic nervous system kicks in. The parasympathetic nervous system returns the organs to their original functionality, slows the heart rate, and returns blood circulation to normal.

But what if the stressors never diminish and you find yourself in a constant state of stress? You will likely end up with one of the many stress-related physical and psychological problems that are epidemic to our society.

So it is in your best interest to do everything you can to reduce your stress response. How can you do this? Read on. In the remainder of this chapter, you will find information and exercises that will help you break the vicious cycle of stress response in your life.

practice Know Thyself

One way to gain control over your stress response is to realize when it has become inappropriate. Some stress is beneficial, but when and how does it become a problem for you? One way to determine this is to watch your physical body closely. Often, even before your conscious mind becomes aware of a stressor, the muscles in your body respond to it, becoming tense and rigid.

If you are under the influence of chronic stress, you probably have a few stress-related knots around your neck and shoulders. Sound familiar? Work to release these knots through stretching, massage, and breathing exercises such as those in the following chapters. Be patient—your body has a stress habit, so these tense spots may take awhile to alleviate.

Also, notice how your body responds when you are in a highly stressful situation. Do you hold your shoulders high? Does your breathing become shallow and rapid? These little details can be your clue to the point at which stress hormones have gone from helpful to hurtful.

Use All Your Senses

Your brain is designed to accommodate at least five senses—sight, touch, sound, smell, and taste. But how much do you really engage all five? Take, for example, the simple act of eating. When you eat, of course you notice the taste of the food, but do you fully utilize the rest of the senses? Do you take time to feel and appreciate a full range of tastes, textures, and smells in your food?

The way most of us take in sensory input is a little like eating a steady diet of fast food. Typical fast-food fare, consisting of ground meat, refined wheat flour, processed cheese, and frozen and refried potatoes, deprives you of sensory range. The natural texture of this meal has been removed to produce an even, comfortable mouth feel that requires as little chewing as it does mental adjustment.

Maybe you are already wise enough to avoid the fast-food trap, but could you be living a fast-food existence through your brain? Just as some people turn repeatedly to a favorite fast-food comfort meal, your brain may have developed a fast-food sensory habit.

In the case of a fast-food meal, one has sacrificed other sensual elements in favor of one—flavor. Consider how you may be doing the same with your other senses. People today are prone to rely on one sense, especially visual stimuli, at the expense of the others. When asked to describe some object, what do you focus on? Chances are that you describe how it looks, but usually not how it feels or sounds or tastes. In most experiences, one sense comes to the forefront while the others blur into the background.

Through this habit, you deny the many parts of the brain involved with sensory processing the chance to work in tandem and to open up new modes of experience for you. One very quick way to build additional connections in the brain is to simply open up your senses fully to the world around you.

Life is like a beautiful feast. Take the time to open yourself to the full range of experiences it offers.

practice Wide-Awake Walking

Walking is a fabulous exercise for many reasons. Regular walking reduces the occurrence of many common diseases and contributes to a general sense of well-being. These benefits are probably no surprise to you, but did you know that walking is also good for your brain?

Many areas of the brain work together to facilitate this commonplace, yet remarkable, activity. Just the act of walking in itself is like a great wake-up call for the brain. In fact, many famous artists, philosophers, writers, and musicians, including Charles Dickens, Wolfgang Amadeus Mozart, and Thomas Jefferson included walking as part of their method of finding inspiration. It seems that the complex mechanism of walking touches on many parts of the brain and allows ideas to flow in new and exciting ways.

So use walking as a way to awaken your brain and find inspiration for your life as well. As you walk, make a point of engaging all of your senses fully. Most of us tend to rely primarily on the sense of sight, so make a point of using your ears, nose, and skin as well. Take in all the layers of sound, smell the many fragrant odors of the day, and feel every part of your body as you move through the air.

Move Your Body

Muscles in your body atrophy without use. Likewise, you must use your brain to keep it functioning at full capacity. Fortunately, you can kill two birds with one stone by moving your body. Every time you exercise your muscles, you are also exercising your brain.

The brain-related benefits of exercise are well documented. Even very simple muscle movements have been found to prompt the growth of cells in the brain. Regular aerobic exercise is known to accelerate memory recall, increase endorphins, reduce depression, shorten reaction time, and circulate more oxygen to the brain.

Exercise helps create the ideal conditions for brain development within your body. First, it helps to reduce the effects of stress by neutralizing stress hormones and by stimulating the sympathetic nervous system. Secondly, it improves the overall efficiency of your cardiovascular system, which in turn brings more blood and oxygen to the brain.

Not only does regular exercise create a healthier bodily environment for nerve cells, but the actions themselves stimulate new growth. Every time you move your body, corresponding areas of your brain are activated. If the action is complex, involving the coordination of muscles, balance, and sense, such as in the act of walking, many areas of your brain will be activated simultaneously. As a result, new growth will be stimulated and old connections between disparate parts of the brain will be solidified.

For best utilization of the brain, look for novel, unexpected ways to move the body. Our tendency can be to only move the body in habitual ways. Even people who exercise regularly tend to return to the same activities over and over again. Instead, try cross training the brain, just as an athlete might cross train the body for better results. Also, look for exercises that move the body in a variety of directions, such as yoga or dance, as opposed to exercise that uses the same repetitive motions.

Regular exercise will also give you the strength and stamina you need to act on the creative inspiration produced by your brain. Without this basic form of health, you may find yourself too tired and unmotivated to act upon your dreams. Furthermore, physical training helps develop the self-control, integrity, and willpower you will need to begin creating the life of your dreams.

 **practice** Stretch It Out

When you wake up, what is the first thing you usually do? Most people yawn and stretch their bodies. Even small children do this without ever being taught to do so. Even cats and dogs stretch. Instinctively, the brain knows that the body must move for the brain to become fully in gear. When you stretch, it is like a million ignition switches have been turned on that tell the brain, "Let's get ready to go!"

There is no reason that this same principle cannot be applied to your brain at any time of the day. Especially if you have a job that is sedentary, your brain can be lulled into brain wave activity that is similar to sleep. You have probably experienced this as sleepiness or a general brain fog. To avoid this, get up from your chair at regular intervals and stretch your body.

When you are engaged in a sedentary activity, such as computer work or book study, stop once every hour or so to stretch your body. Start with the neck and shoulders and work your way down to the leg muscles and feet. Try to move the muscles in all directions. Breathe in as you hold the stretch for about five seconds, and then release as you exhale. Soon, your blood will be circulating more effectively throughout your body, delivering fresh oxygen to your tired brain.

Center Yourself

Several studies have shown that very specific, concrete things happen in the brain when you meditate. During meditation brain waves resemble those seen when someone is asleep and dreaming. But, unlike when you are asleep, you are fully conscious when you meditate. You could look at meditation as a kind of waking sleep, a time when you have consciously and purposely allowed your brain to rest and relax deeply.

Meditation could be described as happiness training. Dr. Richard Davidson of the University of Wisconsin theorizes that meditation increases activity in the left prefrontal cortex, which is associated with feelings of contentment and joy. The more you practice meditation, the more your brain will gain the habit of using these regions of the brain. Also, scientists have noted that meditation calms activity in the amygdala, which is responsible for fear and stress responses.

Research confirms that meditation has surprisingly profound effects on the structure and function of the brain. In one study of Buddhist monks, who usually meditate for many hours a day, the cortical regions of the monks' brains were found to be much thicker than average, suggesting a much greater capacity for deep concentration. Furthermore, the monks showed greater activity in the areas of the brain associated with happiness, something we all want for our lives.

practice Blind Balance

Balancing exercises are a great way to practice finding your center in your body. In a way, you can look at them as a meditation for the body. To begin, balance on your right foot while bending your left knee and bringing your left foot up to your right knee. Make fists and hold your arms at your waist. See how long you can hold this posture. Switch and try the same thing on the other foot.

Once you can hold the pose on each foot for at least twenty seconds, try the same thing again, but with your eyes closed. If you find it is difficult to balance with your eyes closed, it means you are not finding your center within your body. Rather, you are relying on outside information, which you take in through your eyes, to help you keep balanced. Make a point of focusing two inches below your belly button, which is the center of the physical body. You might even want to tap the area with your fingertips. Keep practicing until you can stand at least one minute without opening your eyes.

Breathe Well

Breathing is essential to brain health. Without the oxygen it provides, your brain cannot live for more than a few minutes. With each breath we take, oxygen is dumped into the blood supply, and much of it is eventually used by the brain. Thus, it is important for the health of our brain that we breathe well to keep our blood fully oxygenated.

If you are like a lot of people, you breathe very poorly. You breathe shallowly and use only a small portion of your lung capacity. However, you did not start out this way. When you were a baby, no one had to teach you how to breathe well. You were a natural-born breather. Have you ever watched an infant sleeping? They can teach you a lot about how to breathe well.

When a baby breathes, his or her entire chest and abdomen lifts with each breath. But as we grow older, the effects of stress and improper posture begin to compromise our breathing ability. The chest becomes tight, the abdomen becomes stiff, and we begin to use only our upper chest to breathe. This is a natural reaction to prolonged stress, which results in decreased efficiency in all the organs, including the lungs.

To improve this situation, you can begin to draw more conscious awareness to your breathing. In effect, you need to retrain yourself to breathe as you did when you were a baby. Brain scans have shown that conscious breathing, when compared to unconscious breathing, activates many areas of the brain in addition to oxygenating the blood. Make it a point to notice and correct your own breathing habits.

practice Belly Breathing

Lie down on your back on a flat comfortable surface, such as the floor or a bed. Bring your arms out from your sides about forty-five degrees, and place your feet about shoulder width apart. Focus on relaxing your body completely.

At first, just focus on the rhythm of breath in your chest. Do not try to force your breath; just relax and follow your natural pattern. With every exhalation, try to release more and more tension from the body. Focus on each part of the body, letting go of all tension in that area. Thoroughly release all tension from the face, shoulders, arms, back, abdomen, and feet. When you feel fully relaxed, begin to gently breathe more deeply into the abdomen, until you feel increased warmth in the lower abdomen.

Unify Your Mind and Body

To really learn how to use your brain well, you should consider pursuing some kind of physical training in depth. Through rigorous training of this sort, you will learn to overcome limitations in your body, and your brain will gain the upper hand over the rest of your body. As an added bonus, you will gain increased confidence in many areas of your life.

Any sort of athletic training will help you achieve this, but some sorts of training are especially effective at uniting the mind and body. Many ancient Asian practices, including yoga, tai chi, ki gong, and many martial arts, specifically seek to train the mind in relationship to the body. The word *yoga* means "to unify," and the goal is to bring together the mind and body as one. Numerous studies have confirmed the significant effect these practices can have on your brain to facilitate deep relaxation, improve coordination, and develop focus.

One element that all these practices have in common is the concept of ki (or chi or qi), which is considered to be the life energy that flows through the universe. This element is also the focus of traditional Asian medical practices, such as acupuncture and herbal medicine, which seek to balance and facilitate the flow of ki through the body.

Even though ki may not be as tangible as other biological functions, it is helpful to see energy as the mediator between mind and body. Doing so will help you gain some sense of connection between the two, and it can help you coordinate your body more completely with your brain. When visualizing the brain, it is helpful to think in terms of energy since the entire nervous system incontrovertibly relies on electrochemical impulses to send and receive its messages.

In fact, you may already be accustomed to noticing some link between your brain and energy, even if you don't call it ki. In the most obvious example, you have probably noticed that when your brain is very alert and positive, your energy level is also very high. On the other hand, your energy level drops when your mind sinks into sadness and worry.

These are basic examples of the way that life energy follows the fluctuations of your brain, but you can also look closer at the fluctuations of energy in your body. For example, if you feel tension in your body due to stress, you can view this as stagnant energy. Because you know that energy moves according to the mind, your brain can come to the aid of your body to help release the effects of stress and to gain mastery over your mental and physical health.

🌸 practice Energy Ball

Ki energy cannot be seen, but it can be felt. This exercise will help you learn to sense its presence. Furthermore, it requires deep, relaxed concentration, the perfect remedy for frazzled, stressed-out brains. You should be as relaxed as possible before attempting this exercise, so stretch your body and do some belly breathing (page 31) before you begin.

First, sit in a cross-legged position with your back straight. If this is uncomfortable, use a chair or lean against a wall. Place your hands comfortably on your thighs with your palms facing upward. Close your eyes and relax deeply. Begin to focus on the surface of your palms. Notice any sensation on the palms. You may notice warmth, tingling, or other sensations.

Lift your hands and turn your palms toward each other. Bring them closer together until they are about an inch apart. Again, concentrate on the sensation between the palms, feeling the energy between the palms. Slowly begin to pull your hands apart slightly, keeping your focus on the sensation. Then push your palms slowly back together. Continue this motion, feeling the energy ball grow and shrink.

2.

Flexing Your Gray Matter

At one time, brain scientists believed that once we reached adulthood, the connections in our brains were fixed. More recently, however, the brain has revealed a remarkable ability to rewire itself, which is called neuroplasticity. This is a very hopeful concept since it suggests that we have far more control over our neurological destiny than genetic determinists might suggest. But to take full advantage of this feature, we must get in the habit of rewiring our brains with ease, which is what the second step, **Brain Versatilizing**, is all about.

Surprise Your Brain

Your brain will gain a lot of flexibility if you get in the habit of changing your point of view very quickly. This is critical for creative problem solving, and it will help you manage human relationships better as well.

In fact, many very creative people have developed techniques to force their brains away from the ordinary into the realm of the extraordinary. This may take the form of moving the body in an unusual way or having contact with an unusual object so that many senses and associations are engaged simultaneously. In a way, this simply surprises the brain, getting it out of its rut. You may have noticed that you get your best ideas in the shower or in line at the grocery store, rather than when you are working hard, trying to be creative. Creative ideas rarely come when they "should" because routine and normalcy are the opposite of creativity. Showering and grocery shopping are also ordinary activities, but they do provide a shift in perspective and sensory input away from the typical work environment.

Maybe you imagine a writer spending his or her days behind a desk, sitting in a chair. Robert Louis Stevenson, Mark Twain, and Truman Capote all lay down to write when they were looking for inspiration. Ernest Hemingway, Virginia Woolf, and Lewis Carroll all wrote standing up. William Wordsworth sharpened pencils to find inspiration. And many simply went out for a walk—Henry David Thoreau, A. E. Housman, and Charles Dickens, to name a few.

Essentially, these activities open up your brain to new ways of thinking. They take it outside its normal routine so that more original patterns of thought can be encouraged. So be sure to shake up your routine from time to time to keep your brain vital and fresh.

practice See Both Sides

Think of something nonhuman in your house that you interact with every day. It could be an object, like a TV or a toaster, or maybe a beloved pet. Now, write a complete description of this thing, telling all about how it looks and acts.

Then, write a description of yourself, from the point of view of the object. How do you look from its perspective?

Step Out of Your Comfort Zone

Humans tend to be lazy. They like to do what is easiest. Sadly, though, this is the worst possible thing for the brain.

Let's say you are a college student who gets to choose an elective every semester. Also imagine that you are great in humanities but rotten at math. Which are you going to choose? If you are like most people, you will add an extra humanities course to your schedule.

The humanities course will indeed take less energy than a math course. Not only will you have to study fewer hours, but your brain will not have to exert extra energy to grow the brain connections that make advanced mathematical reasoning possible.

But which is really best for the brain? Math, of course— the thing that is not so automatic for you. The same would be true for the math whiz—he or she should sign up for a course in writing poetry or something of that sort. If an activity is easy for you, the neural connections needed to execute it are already in place in your brain. There is no real challenge for the brain there. So if you take the humanities class, you are really only reinforcing the already existing pathways. If you really want to grow your brain, try doing the thing you stink at!

Sadly, our culture does not reward those who stick their necks out in this way. It rewards the safe choice instead.

You, as the hypothetical college student, will probably maintain a better GPA if you take the easy course.

I would urge you to reconsider anytime you say to yourself, "I can't do that," or, "I am no good at that." If you can't sing, start belting out songs whenever you get the chance. If you have two left feet, get out there and start dancing the night away. Be unabashed about your inability and magnanimous in the face of your own embarrassment. Your brain will thank you for it, and you might just have a whole lot of fun in the process.

 **practice**

Rock, Paper, Scissors, Brain

There are a number of different hand-coordination exercises that can challenge your brain and help you grow new brain connections. In fact, when children play hand-clapping games, they are doing a lot to help develop their own brains. There is no reason that this sort of self-development play should take place only in a schoolyard, though. Practicing and mastering a variety of hand-coordination games will help keep you in the habit of growing new connections for brain flexibility.

Try this one, which is based on the old Rock, Paper, Scissors game. First, practice making the three motions with both hands until you can do it with either hand very quickly and easily. Then, try doing it with both hands together so that one hand is making the symbol that cancels the other. For example, when the right hand is making the rock symbol, the left is making paper. Continue practicing until you can do this very quickly and fluidly.

Break Your Habits

Aristotle said, "We are what we repeatedly do." In other words, we are our habits. In the case of good habits, this is not a problem. These things continually work in our favor, helping us to live better, more fulfilling lives. But when it comes to bad habits, this is not so great. These can take the form of addictive emotional patterns that disrupt our relationships or poor nutritional habits that undermine our physical health. If you look at your habits very closely, you will see that most of the problems in your life are clearly related to some habit or another.

When viewed from the perspective of the brain, habits are the product of well-established brain connections. When you first do something you would consider a bad habit, let's say biting your fingernails, it is not yet a habit. But for some reason, you feel compelled to repeat this behavior many times. Maybe the nail-biting helps release some nervous tension or staves off your boredom for a while. Whatever the reason, you return to the behavior again and again, with increasing frequency, until you develop a full-blown habit. Every time you return to the action, brain connections are reinforced and solidified, making the behavior very comfortable and automatic for your brain to process. This hardwiring combined with sensations of pleasure result in a newborn habit.

The good news is that the brain's amazing neuroplastic ability will allow you to break bad habits and replace them with a more constructive behavior pattern.

practice 21-Day Challenge

Identify one habit in your life that you think causes some sort of difficulty for you. Ideally, this should be a purely behavioral issue, rather than one with a chemical component, such as smoking or drinking. Give yourself the challenge of stopping the behavior for twenty-one days. At the end of the twenty-one days, your dependence on that behavior will have faded along with the neural connections that support it.

Redefine Creativity

First of all, everyone is a creative person. Sometimes we give only musicians, actors, and other artistic types credit for being creative. This is very unfortunate because creativity is a gift given to every human being, not just a talented few. In actuality, you are creating all the time, whether you are aware of it or not.

It is wonderful to create beautiful paintings or inspiring poems, but true creativity is about creating something far more important than these. The most important thing you create is your life itself. It is critical that you empower yourself to create the life you want. Many people ignore their own creative genius in this regard and turn over the creation of their lives to others. Instead of deliberately creating the life they would like to live, they simply follow the expectations of society, family, or some other influence.

You should ask yourself, "What do I really want?" Once you have found an honest and sincere answer to that question, you can start creating your life accordingly. Don't believe anyone who says you are not good enough or do not deserve the life you want. There may be many obstacles to overcome, but with diligence you can create anything. This, I think, is the true meaning of creativity.

 **practice**

The Architect of Happiness

Imagine that your life is a giant mansion with many rooms. Each room represents some aspect of your life—your job, your relationships, your hobbies, and so forth. How does your life-mansion look from the outside? How does each room look? In what condition are the decorations and furnishings? If you want, draw your house on a large piece of paper.

Now, think about how you would like to remodel your house. Imagine the perfect house, representing your perfect life, clearly in your mind.

Create Your Life

"What do I really want?" is one of the most important questions you can ask yourself. It sounds simple enough, but few people ever answer the question honestly. Our brains become entangled in how we think we should be and in what we want others to think about us. Also, it is hard to look beyond the surface to see our own underlying motivations for life.

I urge you to ask yourself this question very sincerely. And then, ask yourself again. Try to really get to the core of what you want. This will free you from being caught up in the details of what you think you want so you can achieve what you really want.

For example, maybe you would answer the question by saying, among other things, "I want a successful career." But why do you want a successful career? There may be multiple reasons. Maybe you want to feel that you have lived a productive life, maybe you want to feel respected, or maybe you want to be financially secure. Now ask yourself why you want these things. You may discover that you want to find meaning for life through productivity, or that you feel loved when people show you respect and when you are given adequate compensation for your work. Ultimately, you may find that all the things and accomplishments that you desire can be narrowed down to a few specific attributes, such as love or freedom.

Knowing what you really want will give you more options in your quest to find fulfillment because you can free yourself from the notion that particular details must be in place in order for happiness to be achieved.

As you create your life, remember to look at the forest, not the trees. If you get stuck looking at details, expecting them to be just so before you can move toward your dreams, you will probably never truly advance.

practice Foundation of Desire

Make a list of everything you currently desire in your life, from tangible objects to nuances of change in your current relationships. Narrow these things down to the emotions that underlie the desires. Consider ways you could achieve these same things in ways other than those you are currently pursuing.

3. Cleaning Out the Attic

Emotions are the stuff of life. Without them, what would life be? It is hard to imagine life without laughter, excitement, tears, or pain. It would hardly be living at all. When you look closely, it is clear that most of the decisions we make in life are ultimately made for emotional reasons. We want good relationships to feel loved, success to feel respected, and money to feel secure.

But what happens when emotions lead you to make decisions that you regret? And what if some negative emotional memory so entraps you that you no longer fully enjoy your life? Realizing that emotions all come from the brain, and that your brain is yours to use as you wish, is the lesson of the next step, **Brain Refreshing**.

Look Within

When looking at the problems that exist in our lives, the tendency is to look outward. For example, when cataloging your difficulties, you may say, "My coworkers are unsupportive, and my husband just doesn't understand." These sorts of things may be true, but there is very little you can do about them. Trying to make your coworkers more supportive and trying to force your husband to understand will probably only make things worse.

Most people do the same thing with their emotions— they look outward to find the source. Even though you know that emotion actually comes from your brain, you probably say, "This makes me happy," and, "That makes me mad." In actuality, nothing makes you happy or angry. The emotions all come from within you. How you react emotionally is entirely dependent on the set of preconceptions and expectations that exist within you. While you may be able to empathize with others and they with you, ultimately your emotional experience is entirely unique to you.

For example, imagine that two drivers take the same highway home from a vacation on the same day. Both have been driving for ten years and have excellent driving records. One of the drivers says, "That road made me so nervous!" But the other says, "The twists and turns on that highway were exhilarating!" What is really the difference between their two experiences? Did the highway do something to make one driver confident and the other nervous? Of course not.

The difference exists in the internal world of each driver, in the self-reliance and expectation within each driver. More accurate comments about the highway might have been, "I made myself nervous when driving on that road," and, "I looked at the highway as a positive challenge." This is the same sort of choice we face in all of our emotional reactions.

When we look outside ourselves to find the source of our emotions, we essentially give up a great deal of personal power. By looking inside, we can concentrate on the things that we can truly change in a given situation—the part that we have contributed. Even if someone else is responsible for 99 percent of a given problem, the 1 percent that you have control over is the only part you can really affect.

☙ practice Turning It Outside In

Are there conditions in your life that you don't like but that never seem to change no matter how hard you try to make them change? Quit trying to make them change. Instead, see how you can change yourself in relation to the problem. Yes, there are some truly intolerable situations that are genuinely beyond repair. In this worst-case scenario, you can resolve within yourself to leave the situation entirely. But most human problems are not so absolute. More than likely, even small changes that come from within you will completely transform your situation. These can change the way you communicate with others and help you reformulate your methods of coping with problems.

Let Go of the Rubbish

Would you let your trash pile up week after week and year after year? Probably not. You know it's bad for your health, unpleasant, and simply unnecessary.

Yet people do this very thing with their emotions all the time—even though it is unhealthy, unpleasant, and totally unnecessary. They hold on to negative emotional memories from yesterday, last month, and even years ago. Often, they let these things color their experience of the present, allowing them to become part of how they define themselves.

If you find yourself clinging to certain negative emotions, perhaps you are hoping for some resolution that will never come. Maybe you hope those mean kids who taunted you will finally see the light or that you will receive the apology you deserve from your ex. These things might be nice if they were to happen, but they are ultimately out of your control. They are up to those individuals, not up to you.

Research has shown that negative emotions literally shrink the overall mass of the brain and interfere with memory and learning. So develop the habit of releasing emotions quickly as soon as they are no longer useful to you. Your brain will be a lot happier for it.

 **practice**
Breathing Out Emotions

If you find yourself dwelling within a particular emotion, try using breath to let go of the emotion and to deliberately replace it with another more positive emotion. Begin by following the steps for belly breathing, on page 31. Visualize the emotion as part of the tension in your body. You may see it as a dark cloud within you. As you breathe in, imagine that a bright light is piercing through that darkness, the way sunlight cuts through a dark cloud. As you exhale, toxic vapors from the clouds are expelled from your body. Smile gently with each exhalation, allowing the light to overcome the darkness.

Empower Your Smile

If you want to be happy, stop waiting for others to make you happy. Just decide to be happy. If your life seems too dreary, smile anyway.

This may seem like Pollyanna, pie-in-the-sky nonsense at first, but it is very much rooted in the physiological reality of your brain. When you smile, even when it is a forced smile, chemicals associated with happiness are released in the brain. Also, smiling is contagious. Very few people can resist the urge to smile back when you smile at them.

As wonderful as a smile is, laughter is even better. The old saying "Laughter is the best medicine" is literally true. Laughter boosts the immune system and reduces the stress response, and thus is excellent for brain health. Furthermore, good attitude and lots of positive social interaction seem to reduce the risk of dementia and other aging-related brain disorders. A happy brain, it seems, is a healthy brain.

practice Give Smiling a Chance

Do you ever feel like you are the only nonobnoxious person in the universe? Do you find yourself getting a little impatient with people around you? Maybe you fly off the handle when someone cuts you off in traffic, or maybe you snap at that telemarketer who calls during dinner. These are the sorts of reactions that are truly a waste of your energy, because they do nothing to change the situation, and they erode your personal well-being. So give smiling a try instead. Maybe even chuckle a little at yourself. Soon, you will break your habitual reactions, and you will feel a whole lot better inside.

Use Your Emotion Well

The need to get ahold of your emotions does not mean that emotions are bad. Emotions are a little like wild horses. A horse that is not broken to the saddle is out of control and of little use to a rider. But a horse that is under control is both useful and a great companion. The important thing is to master your emotions without letting them master you.

Emotions, like a bucking horse, can be quite formidable and difficult to control. The point is not to eliminate emotions as though they were somehow bad, but rather to gain control of your brain by using emotions in a positive, life-enhancing way. If you use them properly, emotions can become a wellspring of energy for your life.

You may already think you are fully in control of your emotions. After all, you don't have emotional outbursts, and you are good at hiding your emotions. This, however, is more like leaving the horse to itself in the barn. It does not mean you have your emotions under control.

Emotions are a very powerful product of the brain, and it would be a shame to waste their potential. The best use for emotions is to redirect their energy in a constructive way. For example, it is obviously not advisable to act upon anger by yelling or hitting. Nor is it advisable to simply bury the anger inside where it eats away at your health and confidence.

Rather, make a conscious decision to recycle that emotional energy into a constructive form. Let go of your need to show others your emotions, to show them that you are angry or sad or jealous. Instead, ask yourself, "How can I use this emotion well?" And then watch as your anger turns to motivation, your jealousy turns to greater attentiveness, and your sadness turns to compassion.

practice Positive Reinforced

It may be difficult at first to redirect your emotions in a positive direction. You may find yourself returning to the destructive emotion, even after you have made up your mind to change. Remember, though, that it is just a habit of the brain that keeps bringing you back to that point. As with any habit, it will take time and practice to break it.

To keep yourself on the positive track, find a way to remind yourself of the constructive action that will replace the negative emotion. For example, you might want to get a small stone and write an inspiring word on it. Or wear a ring that reminds you of your promise to yourself. Every time you see it, your mind will be redirected in a more positive direction.

Zero In on Nothingness

The best way to become more creative is to create nothing. By this, I mean that you should return to zero point. Rid yourself of all the mental and emotional blocks that keep you from manifesting your full creative potential. These are the preconceptions and emotional memories that prevent you from living your dreams fully.

Ironically, it is your ego that prevents you from creating what you truly want. Your ego says to you, "I am this," or, "I should be that," which often stops you from doing what you really want to do. For example, you may have always wanted to learn to sing well, but your ego says, "I don't have musical talent," or, "I will probably embarrass myself if I sing." These things are usually rooted in your past experiences, times when you were hurt by others or were discouraged in some way. To challenge your brain more, try to let go of these old memories and self-imposed limitations.

True genius is not about retaining a lot of information and performing well on intelligence tests, but rather it is about being able to use that information in unique ways. Anyone can be a genius in some way because everyone possesses creative ability. But you must believe you have limitless potential in order to manifest your genius fully. Tell yourself every day, "I am a genius," and believe it. When such a thought is completely and honestly formed in your mind, you will find that creativity begins to flow naturally from your brain.

So to become more creative, begin to watch the internal conversations you have with yourself. How are you limited and boxed in by your current thinking about yourself? How does it stop you from doing what you really want to do? What emotional patterns prevent you from pursuing your dreams?

Let go of illusions about how to be creative. Many believe that great geniuses get an idea out of the blue one day, and all they have to do is to seize that idea and put it into action. Such is not the case. Before they were able to take off into the sky, the Wright brothers went through hundreds of experiments. For the wing alone, they tried out over two hundred variations.

Be patient in allowing your creativity to blossom. The "aha!" moment of inspiration comes when knowledge, experience, and ideas coalesce; it is the moment the brain connects them. It is crucial to know that until the light bulb in the brain turns on, there must be constant planning, a determined will, and a whole lot of trial and error.

The most important point is to do something. If you have a good idea, you must act on it or it will be meaningless. As you are involved in executing an idea, new ideas will come to you. As you repeat this cycle, solutions to your problems will be found and you will become more creative. Creativity is not the result of chance and luck. Creativity happens through focus, determination, and passion.

✿ practice Seeing in the Raw

Take a walk outdoors and take a careful look at something, maybe a tree or a mailbox—anything stationary will do. Try to experience that object just as it is, without any interpretation from the mind—no judgment, categorization, or emotional association. It will be impossible, really. Because you are a human who has lived a certain amount of time on this planet, you are bound to have numerous associations and judgments about the world around you. You may think, "That tree is beautiful," or, "That mailbox belongs to the Smiths." None of these things are intrinsic to the thing itself; they were placed upon the experience as it was filtered through the content of your brain. Continue to practice separating the real experience of an object from the altered experience, and you will find, at least for brief moments, the unadulterated experience. That is zero point.

4. Connecting the Dots

In the previous chapters, you should have essentially gained a measure of control over the more primitive parts of your brain. By lessening the stress response, for example, you have gained some influence over the basic workings of the brain stem and its regulation of heartbeat, respiration, and so forth. The limbic system also is now more in line with your ideals and aspirations as you learn to control and choose your emotions.

Now it is time to unify these various parts of your brain through the cerebral cortex, which is the thinking and reasoning part of our brain. This step is **Brain Integrating**, the point at which you are ready to redefine yourself and re-create your life according to your dreams.

Seek Fulfillment

Scholar Joseph Campbell used to give his students this simple advice for life: "Follow your bliss." This is very good advice. The trick is to recognize the difference between true happiness and mere excitement. True happiness is lingering, while excitement will tend to fade when the honeymoon is over. Try to find that thing that brings you happiness in a pure, continual way. Not only is happiness good for the brain, but focusing on achieving something of this sort will require you to constantly sharpen the use of your own brain.

Ultimately, this will require action that is connected to your most precious core values. Most people want to leave the world in better condition than they found it, to contribute in some way. You might start by asking yourself, "What does the world really need to make it a better place?" Your answer will reflect your basic values and beliefs. Helping to provide that thing is probably related to your ultimate calling in life.

If you choose your life purpose appropriately, it does not mean that your life will be free of strife. If anything, you will invite difficulty because it will mean taking a less safe, less clearly established path in life. Like the heroes of the ancient epics, your resolve will be tested over and over again. An easy life, of course, is not the same as a fulfilling life, and challenges are fuel to a vital brain.

If you look at the world around you, you will see that there are two directions that life can go. Living things either grow or they decline. Your body is bound to decline one day. But if you choose a path that challenges you to continually refine and develop your mind and spirit, you will provide yourself with a lifetime of growth and fulfillment.

 **practice**

What the World Needs Now

On a piece of paper, write down a list of the values and attributes that are most desperately needed in the world. To what extent are you currently helping to provide these to the world? Is there more you can do to help provide these?

Choose Your Identity

People tend to think they are born into their identity as though it were written into their genetic code upon conception. In reality, though, identity is a mental construct. Your identity is invented in your head, or you adopt it from others who invented it for you. Breaking this illusion of identity may be one of the most important things you can do in the quest to become the true master of your own brain.

When you were a small child, you may have had a clearer picture of who you wanted to be. You simply wanted to be one of the good guys who were nice to others and did something helpful with their lives. But as you grew up and experienced life, you added layers on top of that desired identity. These are the ways you choose to present yourself to others, and the way you choose to define who you are to yourself. You accepted a lot of notions about who you are from your environment because you wanted to be loved and accepted. As you became an adult, you added additional layers of your own invention because you wanted to present yourself to your best advantage among your peers and in society at large.

While many of these layers do help us function in society and give us a reference point from which we can estimate our place in the world, they can hold us back from what we truly want to be.

To start peeling these layers back, always ask how and why you created a particular notion about yourself. If you say, "I am no good at math," or, "I am a shy person," ask yourself how and why you took this identity upon yourself. You will find that many of these identities are related to emotional memories that may or may not be serving you well. You may decide to keep those which are beneficial to you and to discard those which are not.

While it may be true that some tendencies are genetically hardwired into our brains, it is up to you whether or not you follow your simple biology. The more you take control of the things you are and the things you will become, the more satisfied and confident you will be within yourself.

practice Corporeal Identity

All sorts of organizations and corporations have slogans: "Be all you can be," "I'm lovin' it," "Just do it." The best ones are simple, concise, and speak volumes about the entities they represent. They say a lot about the way companies view their customers and much about how they want the outside world to relate to them. So why not write a slogan for yourself? It will focus your brain on what you really want to be and maybe help you live up to that ideal.

Set a Lofty Goal

In the East, we have a saying: "Where the mind goes, energy follows." You can see that this is true in just about every human endeavor. Every human achievement, from the most magnificent architectural wonder to the most amazing technological instrument, first came as an idea within someone's brain. After that initial thought, that person or a group of people had to continually focus their mental and physical energy toward the making of that idea into physical form. If they had not, it would have remained just a thought that passed through a person's brain without consequence.

In achieving your goals, you need the same sort of will and determination that built the Seven Wonders of the World. The great builders, thinkers, and artists of the world were not content to think small, and neither should you be.

You should not be afraid to set your goals in life very high. Your vision of who you want to be in this world should fill you with a sense of profound joy. Don't base your goals merely on what you think is safe, or on what others approve of or admire. When you picture your future, you should see the highest, most amazing version of you that you can possibly imagine. If you hold this vision dear to your heart and work toward it continuously, you will always be moving onward and upward in your life.

⚘ practice Vision Meditation

Meditation and prayer are very similar. Both are about very concentrated mind energy. In the case of meditation, there may be no objective other than to empty one's mind, while prayer usually involves some intended outward result. But meditation can also have an objective, and this type of meditation may be more advantageous for the practitioner as a means of clearing away unnecessary clutter from the mind.

Sit in a comfortable chair that has a relatively straight back. Make your back comfortable, but keep it as straight as possible. Also make your legs comfortable; use a footrest if your feet do not easily touch the floor. Breathe deeply and relax the body completely. Remember, in a meditative state, you are fully conscious but as relaxed as when you are asleep.

Take several minutes to make sure that you are fully relaxed, but not dozing. Now take yourself on an imaginary journey through your future, visualizing each remaining year of your life, until you see yourself in your highest form.

Plan for Success

Sometimes a person is called an overnight success, but this is always inaccurate. It may appear from the outside that something big was achieved instantaneously, but that is because the hard work that goes on behind the scenes is often not readily apparent.

In order to achieve anything, you need to have a clear plan to get there, and you must have the patience to carry it out. As the old proverb states, "A journey of a thousand miles begins with a single step." To achieve anything, you must be willing to take each step one at a time.

The trick is to enjoy the present moment while keeping an eye toward the future. If your mind is too consumed by the glorious image you see in the future, you will not be able to focus on your present problems and challenges. And you will have a hard time getting past them.

Your big vision is not really what you should be working on right now. Rather, you should work on the steps that lead to that dream. View these steps as minivisions and take joy in your small successes. Before you know it, all your little steps will add up to one beautiful journey.

practice
PDCA (Plan, Do, Check, Act)

The PDCA method was first created in the 1950s by W. Edwards Deming to help companies improve customer satisfaction. It can also be applied to the achievement of your personal goals by breaking them down into realistic, manageable steps. It also gives you a way to measure your progress.

It is best to begin the PDCA planning process with the end result in mind. From there, work backward through time to create an achievable, step-by-step plan for your growth. What would you like to achieve in the next year? What can you do in one month to move your life closer to your dreams?

Once you have narrowed your vision to a very specific, obtainable one-year goal, you can continue to break it down further into monthly, weekly, and daily PDCA steps. This is your P, your plan. Then, of course, you must do (D). After that, check (C) to see if your plan is really moving you toward your goal. Then, after revising your plan, act (A) again, continually cycling through the PDCA process.

Be Truthful

Once you have really clarified for yourself your new identity, you must work diligently to stay true to it. This is more easily said than done. There may be many forces at play that would like to redefine your new identity.

Some of those forces come from outside of you. There may be many people who are invested in having you act and think in the way that suits them. Of course, if you go along with these forces, you are not managing your own brain at all. You are letting someone else manage it for you.

The most formidable opponent to your true identity, however, may come from within yourself. This is called your ego. Your ego is not a bad thing in itself; it is there to ensure your physical happiness in life. But your ego does not want you to take an unusual path because it is far less comfortable. From your ego's point of view, it is far better for you to take a safe route in life that ensures basic security and status within society. To avoid the pitfalls of the ego, try to recognize when your need for control, recognition, or security has taken over.

 **practice**
The Ritual of Self-Reflection

To remain true to yourself, you must gain the habit of reflecting on the choices you have made. This is very difficult to do in the midst of the whirlwind of life, so it is best to find a quiet time to do this regularly, perhaps early in the morning or just before bed. This could take the form of quiet, meditative contemplation or journaling. As you reflect upon your day, examine each moment you can recall in relation to your highest identity, asking whether your behaviors are in sync with your ideals and are leading you to grow into the person you really want to be.

5.

Seeing the Big Picture

Once you have begun to take control over the internal workings of your brain, it is time to turn the power of your brain outward once again. In short, it is time to act. Through action, you will put all that you have learned through the previous four steps to the test, and you will hone and strengthen their effectiveness. Now is the time to build the life of your dreams through **Brain Mastering**.

View Obstacles as Blessings

No matter how enthusiastic and confident you are about the attainment of your dreams, difficulties will arise. For a lot of people, these obstacles derail their dreams. Somehow, they have developed a fairy-tale idea about how their lives should go. They think that if something is meant to happen it will happen automatically.

Actually, that is not the way of life at all. Just look around you and notice the natural world. Everything is pushing and struggling to move forward. All the beautiful things on this planet came into being as the result of many years, sometimes millions of years, of suffering and strife. Actually, we modern humans have it very easy, being able to accomplish quite a lot in a short life span while living in relative safety and comfort.

Have you ever seen a dandelion pushing itself up through a crack in the concrete? You need to adopt the same mindset if you really want to blossom in this life.

 **practice**

Counting Your Other Blessings

You have probably been told at some time in your life to count your blessings. But have you considered that *everything* in your life is a blessing? Think of a difficult period in your life that has passed or a giant obstacle you have overcome. Consider how that event ultimately was a blessing to you.

Step Beyond Your Limits

It is absolutely true that you have limitations. But you are also limitless. If that seems contradictory, think of your limitations not as brick walls, but rather as soft, plastic structures. Yes, they will slow you down and even stop you for a while, but they can be infinitely pushed and stretched out until they are barely visible at all.

When dealing with your own limitations, don't attempt to jump past them. This approach will probably only create hardship for you. Rather, be very honest and realistic about what they are, and try to go just a tad beyond them each time you face them.

Let's say, for example, that you have always wanted to become a medical doctor. In college, however, you shied away from the premed program because you did horribly in your high school chemistry class, and you dread the chemistry classes that are part of the premed curriculum. In this case, your fear of the chemistry classes and your lack of understanding of the subject matter constitute the limitations concocted by your brain.

Should this limitation make you give up on your dream? Certainly not. Yet these are the very sorts of things that do derail people's dreams. If becoming a doctor is what you really want, then nothing else will ever satisfy you, and you must follow that dream. Set your mind to that goal, and welcome the challenges that come.

As the old saying goes, "Where there is a will, there is a way." In terms of brain management, this means finding the way that your brain is able to do something. Okay, so your brain didn't take very well to chemistry the way it was taught in high school. So what? Find the way your brain can learn it. Try tutors, try study aids, do everything except quit. Eventually, your brain will figure out the appropriate method, and it is at that point that you have stretched your limitations so far that you stepped right over them.

 **practice**
Push-up Your Confidence

Physical fitness training is a good way to gain practice in stepping past limitations. The limitations of the body are clearly defined, and it is clear when we have overcome them. Push-ups are a good example. At first, you will probably only be able to do a few push-ups. Promise yourself that you will add at least one push-up every day. Set a goal of doing a hundred push-ups without stopping. With diligence, you will achieve this very quickly, and you will set precedents for success in all areas of your life.

Develop a Lofty Character

As you move toward your goal, remember that no one is going to hand success to you on a silver platter. It will only come through diligent hard work and continuous refinement of your character. These things, in a way, are more important than achieving the goal itself.

A diamond is just a lump of coal until it is turned into a diamond through constant pressure. You also can be transformed by the pressures you face. Rather than becoming discouraged or destroyed by them, let them shape you into a stronger, more refined human being. Like a diamond, you can gain amazing durability while also remaining pure.

In fact, true greatness in life is really a matter of character. Many people have achieved fame and fortune of some sort. But what makes a person truly great? What makes a Mahatma Gandhi or a Martin Luther King Jr. stand out among people? If you look closely, you will see that the only significant difference is character. On the bodily level, they were no different than ordinary people. They were composed of ordinary flesh and bone, and they did not possess any special superpowers. Even their brains were just ordinary brains. But they used those brains with an astounding level of pure conviction that transformed their characters beyond the ordinary plane of human existence.

To use your brain to its fullest potential, you must develop a similar level of conviction about what you want to contribute to the world. Then, like a cut diamond that sparkles from every angle, you will radiate pure light to everyone you meet.

practice Brain Supermodels

Even grown-ups need role models to look up to. They are yet another way we can help focus our mind toward what we want to become. If you find that you need to develop some specific character trait, choose some iconic person who you think exemplifies that trait, and use him or her as a model. Your brain will respond well to this because the human brain contains many thousand mirror cells, which allow you to learn easily just by watching others. So if you need more courage, you might focus on Amelia Earhart. Or, if you want to exhibit more selflessness toward others, learn all about Mother Teresa. You might read a biography or watch a documentary about the person. Let your hero's life become a metaphor by which you live your own life, and your own greatness will be ignited within your brain.

Trust Your Brain

Only you, and no one else, can erase the limitations in your brain. If you think, "These are my fixed limits," your brain will not try to work beyond those limits. Your brain follows your mind, not the other way around. That is why you must develop absolute trust in your brain to follow your wishes, believing that it has the power to help you move past any limitation or difficulty. Trying to achieve anything substantial without complete trust in your brain is like driving a car with the parking brake engaged and then complaining about not being able to go as fast as you'd like.

If you ask it to, your brain can do things you've never done, even things you are unaware of. Your brain has great power to find and create solutions that are not immediately obvious. However, most people live within the limits of the lives they have experienced and known. They don't know what they haven't learned, they are uninterested in things that are "none of their business," and they fear attempting things outside the scope of their own knowledge and experience. These people do not trust their brains to comprehend anything beyond the usual, and thus their potential is continually truncated.

We are living in an information age, where facts and figures are available at the touch of a button. No longer can people's worth be determined by the information they do or do not hold within their brains. Rather, how information is used is all that really matters.

To gain true trust in your brain, make a point of going outside your existing scope. In other words, quit looking for the same old answers in the same old places. Be unafraid to ask your brain tough questions about the nature of your life and its ultimate meaning. Demand that your brain think outside the box to find new, more effective solutions, and use it to form new, more effective priorities. This is the kind of confidence that will truly transform your life.

✸ practice Alternate Uses

It is important to gain the habit of looking beyond the ordinary, even in the mundane routines of life. To practice this, try looking at the things around you in different ways. For example, look at all the tools and utensils that you have in your kitchen. You have many things—spatulas, knives, pots, and pans—all with specific uses.

To get your brain in the habit of looking beyond the ordinary, list in your mind all the possible alternate uses. For example, perhaps an egg beater could be used to help arrange flowers or as a backscratcher. Challenge your mind in this way as you look around at other objects in your house as well.

Play Well with Others

Always remember that no brain is an island. You cannot really say you are using your brain well if you cannot learn to use your brain in cooperation with other brains. Fortunately, doing this is really not so hard. All you have to do is play well with the other brains, just like you learned in the schoolyard.

Part of the reason that there is so much violence in the world is that some of the most powerful brains in the world believe they should be able to control the information in other brains. Thus, many of the wars and atrocities of history have been justified through ideology and religion.

The same thing happens on a more personal level, too. Husbands and wives try to control the content of the other's brain; parents judge their children's brains and children judge their parents'; even friends fall out over differences of opinion. Your relationships will inevitably crumble if you cannot give up controlling the way other people's brains operate. It may seem like a strange way of putting it, but mutual brain-appreciation is the key to peace on every level.

So rather than attempting to control the brains around you, seek simply to play fairly. Instead of trying to change others, realize that you are responsible only for your own brain, and learn to take joy in the marvelous diversity exhibited through the human brain.

practice Peace Is Possible

It is critical to believe that a peaceful, sustainable way of living is possible for humanity. Many will tell you that this is a pipe dream that will never be achieved. But you must resist that sort of thinking because as long as people think this way, things will always remain as they are. If the mass of humanity continues to believe that human nature is basically self-centered and that there is no way we can change, then that is exactly how things will play out. The most important thing you can do for the Earth is to believe in the marvelous transformative power of the human brain and act accordingly.

The Five Steps of BEST

Brain Education System Training (BEST) is designed to be a simple and easy-to-follow way to maximize your brain potential so you can live a healthy, happy, and peaceful life. The training system is divided into five steps, each one building on the effectiveness of the last. Generally, the steps are practiced in order as you progress through the BEST 5 programs, but they will require continuous practice, and many of the training programs utilize various steps simultaneously and do not necessarily need to be completed in order. For additional information about the theoretical basis of each step, see "BEST 5 Philosophical and Scientific Background" on page 93.

Brain Sensitizing

In this first step, you become very aware of your brain and its importance in your life. Much of the work is done on the physical level since the connection between body and brain is strengthened at this point. Yoga, tai chi, ki gong, and martial arts are examples of mind-body exercises used to establish Brain Sensitizing. As each muscle in your body is moved and every nerve stimulated, corresponding areas of the brain are also awakened. As a result, balance and coordination in your body are improved.

Basic meditation and energy sensitivity techniques are also recommended at this stage as these will help you to develop better concentration and heightened awareness. By learning to view ki energy as the source of communication between body and brain, you are empowered to begin changing habits that negatively affect your body and mind. Breath work is also used to help restore energetic balance while releasing stress and restoring mental clarity.

Brain Versatilizing

Just as the muscles of the body need to be moved and stretched to become flexible, so does the brain. This step seeks to take full advantage of neuroplasticity, the ability of the brain to adjust to new environments and to learn new things. By challenging your brain to master new tasks, you help it gain new connections and greater capacity to recognize new patterns of

[Brain Education 5 Steps]

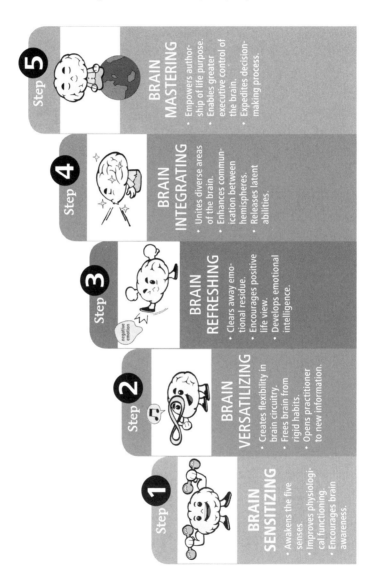

thought and action. Essentially, the goal is to create a highly adaptable brain that can learn quickly and easily.

This step is likely to have a profound effect on the quality of your life because you will learn to break destructive mental and physical patterns of behavior while creating new, life-affirming habits. Bad habits can be difficult to break because they become, to some degree, hardwired into the brain through repetition, which solidifies neural connections related to the behavior. Fortunately, the brain never loses the ability to restructure itself, and thus new connections and habits can always be created. At the most advanced level of training, this includes the ability to change deeply ingrained prejudices and preconceptions for the creation of a better, more satisfying life.

Brain Refreshing

In some ways, this step is a rebirth for the brain. Throughout your life, you have experienced things that have had a lasting effect on your brain. These things linger on as a kind of emotional residue that affects your life. From this residue, you may have created the preconceptions and negative thought patterns that have kept you from reaching your full potential. The intention of Brain Refreshing is to release and clear away these burdensome memories to allow healing and renewal.

Through expressing and releasing old emotions rooted in the traumatic experiences of the past, you will learn to control the content of your own mind rather than being controlled by the whims of emotional variation. You will learn to use the energy of your mind in a more concentrated and uninterrupted way.

Brain Integrating

After you have learned to empty yourself of emotional baggage, you will be ready to expand your awareness and transcend the boundaries of the ego, feeling the oneness of all things. You will be ready to ask yourself fundamental questions about life with complete honesty and sincerity. You will then accept new, positive information into the brain.

Because identity is the core information affecting your life, it is of primary concern, and you can create a new identity based on your newly discovered life purpose. Once you are fully integrated with this new identity, creative potential becomes practically unlimited.

This stage is called Brain Integrating because all layers of the brain are working together and the brain stem is now activated. Also, the left and right hemispheres of the brain begin to communicate better, and disparate parts of the brain start to work together in full cooperation. Through this deep exploration, you can discover the part of you that is truly meant to be in charge of your brain.

Brain Mastering

Now that you have discovered the life you truly want to live, you are ready to create a lifestyle based on the goals that develop through understanding that purpose. This is essentially a spiritual quest because it requires continuous attention to, and development of, the highest aspects of your character. Brain Mastering cultivates the habit of continuous enlightened living as opposed to brief, transient moments of enlightenment.

Through the process of Brain Mastering, your brain will continue to transform and solidify neural connections that support the creation of a truly happy life. Increasingly, your brain will be able to find creative, workable solutions to the basic problems of life. Also, you will become more naturally decisive, and your mind will develop the habit of forming more peaceful relationships with other people and the world as a whole.

BEST 5
Philosophical and Scientific
Background

For ages, people have debated the true nature of the mind and its relationship to the body. Is the mind separate from the body, or does it arise from some anatomically definable place? Are the brain and the mind the same thing? If the mind is only a product of the physical organ of the brain, then why do people have a sense of being more than a mere biological machine?

An Uncomfortable Meeting of Minds

Many in the Western world have somewhat tenuously settled on the dualist idea of the Cartesian split, the concept that the mind and body, while having influence over one another, are distinct entities with distinct attributes. In the Descartes model, the brain is the seat of intelligence and awareness, but the mind itself is clearly distinct from the physical body. This mode of thinking about the mind and body is typical of most

APPENDIX

major religions (e.g., in the belief that the soul outlives the body) and can be traced back to the ancient philosophical writings of Plato and Aristotle.

The modern scientific community, however, does not so easily accept this dualistic notion. The natural tendency of the scientific mind is to rely on the evidence available on the material plane, since that is what can be measured and evaluated. This has led to a more mechanical view of the brain and behavior that sees the brain as the bodily organ responsible for all human perception and experience. Thus, neuroscientists focus mainly on the mechanics of synaptic function and the details of brain anatomy and their relation to various mental processes. This approach has been called materialism. It is a rejection of dualism, insofar as materialists consider all phenomena, including mental processes, to be reducible to some physical activity.

The Easy Problem and the Hard Problem

A mechanical view of the brain is not satisfactory to everyone, however. Philosopher David J. Chalmers has said that the mysteries of human consciousness bring up two fundamental issues—the "easy" problem and the "hard" problem. The easy problem involves describing the physiological source of awareness—for example, pinpointing the locations in the brain related to cognitive processes, and mapping the biomechanical underpinnings of the brain. Most neuroscientific discoveries contribute to solving this easy question.

The hard question, on the other hand, is more slippery. It asks, "Why do we have awareness of our awareness, and what is the ultimate source of that awareness?" A diehard scientific materialist might say that there is no hard question, that there is only mechanical/biological function, but that does not help explain experience. For example, it is true that the color red is created by a particular frequency of the electromagnetic spectrum, but nothing in that frequency can explain why we subjectively experience red as red. Furthermore, a purely materialistic view of the brain leads us to discard choice and free will as illusions.

BEST Perspective

Like the materialistic neuroscientists, the BEST method assumes that understanding and devoloping the brain are critical to improving the human condition.

To train the brain is to train the mind; to understand the brain is to understand the mind. However, in contrast to the purely materialist view, BEST views choice as a fundamental determinant of human life. The condition of the brain may influence our choices, but through BEST, we can also make choices that upgrade our brain activity.

Furthermore, the BEST brain philosophy considers science to be a good servant but a poor master. BEST is rooted in the Eastern principle of Tao, which supposes that all things are one, and all differentiation is an illusion. Tao philosophy encourages individuals to align their thoughts and actions so as to be harmonious with all of humanity and nature. In contrast, the pure scientist sees the universe in terms of randomness and impersonal physical laws. This view leads one to the uncomfortable conclusion that life itself has no intrinsic meaning but, rather, is a competition among selfish genes for perpetuity.

The Source of Inspiration

Recently, much attention has been given to identifying the areas of the brain associated with mystical or spiritual experience. This has led some to conclude that belief in God and other spiritual phenomena is actually hardwired into the brain. In other words, they think that the physical brain is the only reality involved in consciousness, and that soul or spirit has nothing to do with it. Looking at this same data, BEST instructors have come to a very different conclusion: the brain is a divine instrument of interaction between the spiritual, physical, and energetic realms.

These questions about the ultimate nature of human experience are more than bothersome conundrums of scientific and philosophical inquiry; they are some of the most fundamental questions of life itself. This is why BEST practitioners are encouraged to ask themselves, "Who am I?"

This simple question of identity is the one that can ultimately lead to the state defined in Eastern thought as "enlightenment" because a person who can answer that question honestly and confidently is a happy and fulfilled individual. The BEST 5 programs exist to help people investigate possible answers to this question and to define for themselves their true identity—what they really are and what this human life is all about.

East Meets West

Although rooted in ancient Eastern thought, the BEST 5 program boldly seeks to integrate that which is best in both Eastern and Western thought. We see no contradiction in living life according to the principles of Tao, while valuing and using the discoveries of scientific research. We believe that the mystical and the rational, the esoteric and the scientific, ultimately come together as one.

As brain philosophers and brain educators, BEST 5 instructors do not wait for the rigors of science to "prove" the efficacy of any particular exercise. Time is short, and the condition of humanity is dire. The intention of BEST is to bring greater health, happiness, and peace to humanity in this lifetime, and the experiences of BEST practitioners continue to solidify our belief in the profound usefulness of these methods. BEST 5 is a philosophically based educational method that will continually refine itself as our experience and understanding grow broader and deeper.

Debates about the nature of mind aside, the more concrete physical benefits of the BEST 5 approach are clear. The physiological effects of the first BEST step, Brain Sensitizing, are perhaps the most easily understood. Practitioners can verify the effects through their own experience very early in the training process. For example, they may notice improved circulation as their hands and feet become warm for the first time in years, or they may feel more energized and awake throughout the day.

Concrete Benefits of BEST

In a study conducted at Weill Medical College of Cornell University, Dr. Sung Lee studied the outcomes for practitioners who had taken the Dahn Yoga regular class for three months. The participants were surveyed in eight areas related to quality of life, ranging from general health to social and mental well-being. The practitioners improved significantly in all areas measured, including self-efficacy, the critical can-do spirit.

These remarkable results are probably due to the effect of Dahn Yoga on the body's stress response, which is one of the main reasons people seek the BEST 5 training method in the first place. And this is a very good reason to seek training since over-activated stress responses seem to contribute to many modern ailments, including auto-immune diseases, heart disease, weight gain, and high blood pressure.

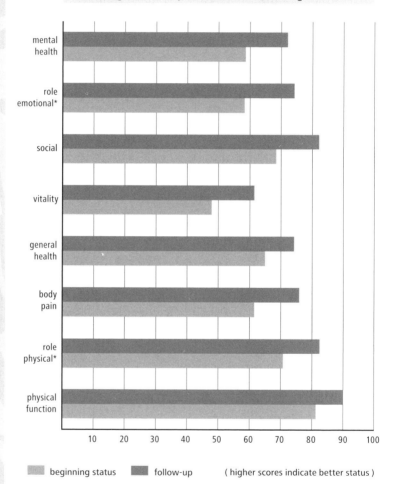

Baseline and three-month follow-up scores for quality of life among new BEST practitioners at Dahn Yoga Centers

- mental health
- role emotional*
- social
- vitality
- general health
- body pain
- role physical*
- physical function

10 20 30 40 50 60 70 80 90 100

beginning status   follow-up   (higher scores indicate better status)

* Physical and emotional roles refer to participants' impression of their health in relation to their occupational role.

Journal of General Internal Medicine, 2004, Vol. 19

The Role of the Brain

But what does all of this have to do with brain training? Well, the entire stress response begins and ends with the brain, because the brain controls the autonomic nervous system, which encompasses both the sympathetic and parasympathetic nervous systems. When people are under continual stress, the sympathetic, or fight-or-flight, response is activated. Under stressful conditions, the brain secretes hormones that affect most of the major organs of the body. In small doses, these hormones can be helpful for both brain and body function, but over prolonged periods, they can be very damaging.

Like other forms of yoga and meditation, the Dahn Yoga regular class stimulates the parasympathetic, rest-and-digest response, which counteracts the stress response that seems to be over activated in so many people these days. Elements such as Jung-Choong Breathing and Meridian Stretching appear to serve as a kind of workout for the vagus nerve, a key player in the parasympathetic response. The vagus nerve connects the medulla in the brain to most of our critical internal organs. When the parasympathetic response is activated, the ideal energy state of "water up, fire down" is experienced. In this condition, the head is cool and the abdomen warm, and energy circulates continuously throughout the body.

The continuous stress that people experience is rooted in sensory input that over-stimulates the sympathetic response. When we meditate or practice deep breathing, we essentially turn off the brain for a while, which delivers it for a moment from the sensory burnout that has become a typical part of our lives. Multiple studies have confirmed the effectiveness of meditation. In actual fact, the brain is not turned off during meditation, but its lobes associated with the five senses are quieted and the regions associated with happiness and well-being are activated.

The Flexible Brain

Once delivered from the ravages of continuous stress, practitioners are ready for the next step, Brain Versatilizing. This step takes advantage of the fact that the brain possesses a remarkable ability, called neuroplasticity, to restructure and reorganize itself. At one time it was thought that the adult brain is more or less hardwired, but now it's clear that people possess the ability to create new brain connections until the end of life. This means that we never lose the ability to learn new things and change our personal habits in whatever way we choose.

This does not always mean, however, that change is always easy. The brain strengthens neural connections whenever we repeat a behavior, so habits can become quite entrenched in the brain, even when we know cognitively that the behavior is not advantageous. The exercises and programs in this step help free individuals from emotional and physical habits by accentuating the neuroplasticity of the brain.

The Emotional Brain

Rewiring the brain can be especially difficult when emotional memory is involved. Essentially, emotional memories can block your ability to learn new things, and therefore they can truncate potential. If you have ever experienced math anxiety or resisted trying something new for fear of embarrassment, you can easily see how emotions get in the way of learning. Often these blocks are buried deep in the subconscious and take some time to resolve. Brain Refreshing exercises help people identify and eliminate these emotional blocks.

The role of emotions in the brain may be much more far-reaching than the personal limitations they impose. Emotions may also have great social impact. Neuroscientist James LeDoux has been a pioneer in identifying how fear arises in the brain. Not only has he identified the location in the brain where fear is processed, he has also identified the mechanism by which the brain creates habitual fears, such as phobias and prolonged anxiety. In addition, he has described how this can play out on the cultural level, in the form of ingrained prejudices used to justify war and other human rights atrocities.

The Unified Brain

Once your brain has gained some degree of freedom from emotions, stress, and ingrained habits, you are ready to ask the fundamental question mentioned earlier—"Who am I?" While you can ask this question at any time, you will be able to answer it much more accurately if your brain is free from old thought patterns that distort your sense of identity. This state is called Brain Integrating because the three layers of the brain—stem, limbic system, and neocortex—are now ready to work together, rather than in opposition. Interestingly, the layers of the brain reflect humanity's evolutionary history—reptile, mammalian, and primate—and now they can be applied to your own personal evolution.

BEST approaches Brain Integrating as a process occurring in two dimensions: on the horizontal axis of the left and right hemispheres, and on the vertical axis of the brain stem, limbic system, and neocortex. You are probably already aware that you have two distinct halves of the brain, and that one side tends to dominate the other. The left hemisphere is responsible for mental processes such as logic, linear thinking, relational problem solving, and verbal ability. The right hemisphere is associated with intuitive ability, imagination, and spontaneity. Brain Integration attempts to get past the dominance of either hemisphere so that the two sides can work together for maximum capacity.

Just as the brain's two hemispheres can be integrated, so can its three vertical layers—the brain stem, limbic system, and neocortex. Once these three levels are working in harmony, the emotions (limbic system) no longer interfere with creative and rational thinking (neocortex), and the physical body (brain stem) works to support all cognitive functions.

[Layers of the brain]

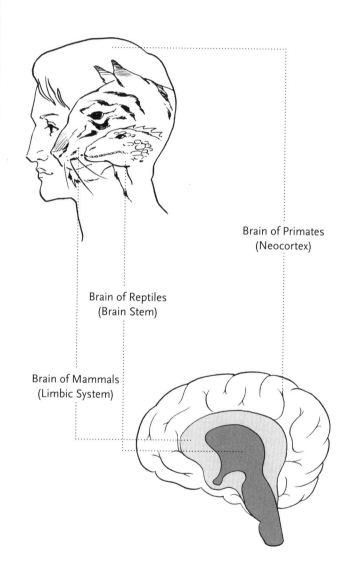

Brain of Primates
(Neocortex)

Brain of Reptiles
(Brain Stem)

Brain of Mammals
(Limbic System)

[left and right brain]

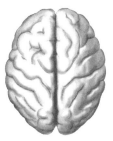

LEFT BRAIN

Logic
Language
Numbers
Details
Analysis
Process

RIGHT BRAIN

Creativity
Imagination
Intuition
Spontaneity
Visualization
Rhythm

The Actualized Brain

The next step involves Brain Mastering, the active development of the frontal lobe—the executive part of the brain that imagines, plans, sets goals, and makes decisions. The goal here parallels Dr. Abraham Maslow's classic psychological model of the self-actualized person. This ideal individual lives life in constant and deliberate self-exploration, continually refining character toward the highest conception of self. Maslow stated emphatically that this self-exploration must be accompanied by action, that it must not become an exercise in self-absorbed introversion. This is why we also advocate following a lofty and worthy vision for one's life.

When creating his model for self-actualization, Maslow drew upon the works of eighteenth-century philosopher Dr. Richard M. Bucke, who advocated the development of what he called "cosmic consciousness." Bucke described this consciousness as the awareness of the world as a giant organism in which one is connected to every living thing. Again, here we see a marvelous parallel to the philosophy of Tao, which stresses the ultimate oneness of all things.

Essentially, the BEST 5 training program is a brain development system that progresses from the physical to the psychological and finally to the philosophical. In the end, it is a life philosophy, a means of continual self-betterment. Our hope is that this system will not only create happiness for individuals, but initiate a wave of health, happiness, and peace throughout the world.

Suggested Reading

Amen, Daniel G. *Change Your Brain, Change Your Life: The Breakthrough Program for Conquering Anxiety, Depression. Obsessiveness, Anger, and Impulsiveness.* New York: Random House, 1998.

Begley, Sharon. *Train Your Mind, Change Your Brain: How a New Science Reveals Our Extraordinary Potential to Transform Ourselves.* New York: Ballantine, 2007.

Bloom, Floyd E., et al, eds. *The DANA Guide to Brain Health.* New York: Free Press, 2003.

Carter, Rita. *Mapping the Mind.* Berkley: University of California Press, 1998.

Damasio, Antonio R. *Descartes' Error: Emotion, Reason, and the Human Brain.* New York: Putnam, 1994.

Doidge, Norman. *The Brain that Changes Itself: Stories of Personal Triumph from the Frontiers of Brain Science.* New York: Viking, 2007.

Howard, Pierce J. *The Owner's Manual for the Brain: Practical Applications from Mind-Brain Research.* 3d ed. Austin: Bard, 2006.

Johnson, Steven. *Mind Wide Open: Your Brain and the Neuroscience of Everyday Life.* New York: Scribner, 2004.

LeDoux, Joseph E. *The Emotional Brain: The Mysterious Underpinnings of Emotional Life.* New York: Touchstone, 1996.
——. *Synaptic Self: How Our Brains Become Who We Are.* New York: Penguin, 2003.

McEwen, Bruce and Elizabeth Norton Lasley. *The End of Stress as We Know It.* Washington, D.C.: DANA, 2004

Pinker, Steven. *How the Mind Works.* New York: Norton, 1997.

Restak, Richard. *Mozart's Brain and the Fighter Pilot: Unleashing Your Brain's Potential.* New York: Crown, 2001.

Sapolsky, Robert M. *Why Zebras Don't Get Ulcers: An Updated Guide to Stress, Stress-related Diseases, and Coping.* New York: Freeman, 1994.

Wilson, David Sloan. *Evolution for Everyone: How Darwin's Theory Can Change the Way We Think About Our Lives.* New York: Delacorte, 2007.

Index

About the Author

For the past twenty-five years, author Ilchi Lee has dedicated his life to finding ways to develop the abilities of the human brain. Brain Education, a mind-body training program that helps to unlock the brain's true potential, is the primary fruit of his search. Through numerous programs for adults and children, many thousands of people have discovered a path to greater health, happiness, and peace.

The ultimate purpose of brain development, according to Lee, is lasting world peace. His Brain-Peace Philosophy identifies the brain as the seat of human consciousness, and therefore it is through developing the brain that he believes humanity may transcend its destructive patterns of violence and hatred.

Currently, Lee serves as the president of the University of Brain Education. Also, he is president of the Korean Institute of Brain Science and chairman of the International Brain Education Association (IBREA). Lee is the author of thirty books. His work as a peacemaker and educator has been widely recognized, both in his native Korea and in the international community.

For more information, please visit www.ilchilee.com and www.ibrea.org.

APPENDIX

Also by This Author

Brain Respiration

Trains the brain using three interrelated and distinct elements: Physical Coordination Exercises for the body, Energy Movement Exercises for the mind, and Awareness Expanding Exercises for the spiritual body. The many concrete benefits of Brain Respiration include: enhanced health, brightened outlook, increased creativity and innovation, heightened academic capability, and improved ability to interact harmoniously with others.

Human Technology

Provides a simple, straightforward guide to personal self-management. Basic skills in meditation, breath work, and Oriental healing arts are presented as an effective means of self-reliant health management. In addition, central issues of life purpose and fulfillment are discussed.

Power Brain Kids

A child-appropriate and parent-friendly guide to Lee's world-renowned Brain Education (BE) method. Each lesson focuses on a particular aspect of mental ability, including concentration, creativity, memory, and emotional control. Through the book, straight-A and struggling students alike will be challenged to apply full brain capacity toward the creation of a genuinely happy and successful life.

Healing Society

A prescription for global enlightenment. The author empha-
sizes throughout the book that enlightenment is not just for
a select few, but available to everyone. He defines enlightenment as "a simple choice that you make to live your life
for the betterment and benefit of all those around you."
One needs only to make that choice, and then develop the
discipline to live out that choice.

The 12 Enlightenments for Healing Society

Inspires readers to "stop seeking enlightenment and start
acting it." Lee shows you how to become what he calls an
"Enlightened Activist" as you push past the artificial boundaries of institutions that prevent you from realizing that
everyone is an Earth Human, a member of a single human
society. Journey toward enlightenment through these twelve
practical, yet spiritual, steps.